THE JAMES BACKHOUSE LECTURES

This is one of a series of annual lectures. The Backhouse Lectures began in 1964 when the Australia Yearly Meeting of the Religious Society of Friends was first established.

The lecture is named after James Backhouse, who travelled with companion George Washington Walker throughout the Australian colonies from 1832 to 1838.

Backhouse and Walker were sent to Australia by the London Society of Friends to investigate and report to authorities on the penal system and on the treatment of aborigines, to promote the cause of temperance and to preach to the scattered settlers both bond and free. The pair travelled to all major centres and to many isolated settlements.

They submitted detailed observations to local as well as British authorities and made recommendations for legislative reform. Many of the changes they initiated resulted in improvements to the health and wellbeing of convicts, Aboriginal people and the general population.

A naturalist and a botanist, James Backhouse is remembered also for his detailed accounts of native vegetation which were later published.

James Backhouse was welcomed by isolated communities and Friends throughout the colonies. He shared with all his concern for social justice and encouraged others in their faith. A number of Quaker meetings began as a result of his visit.

Australian Friends hope that these lectures, which reflect the experiences and ongoing concerns of Friends, may offer fresh insights and be a source of inspiration.

The 2025 Backhouse Lecture "The seed is in all: A journey through the Quaker world" was delivered on 7 July 2025 by Tim Gee, General Secretary of Friends World Committee for Consultation (FWCC), which connects Quakers in different countries.

Tim grew up in a Quaker community in Britain and has previously worked for Britain Yearly Meeting, Christian Aid and Amnesty International. He has written four books: *Counterpower: Making Change Happen* (2011), *You Can't Evict an Idea: What can we learn from Occupy?* (2012), *Why I am a Pacifist* (2018) and *Open for Liberation: An activist reads the Bible* (2022). He contributes regularly to various publications and has been a voice for Quakers on the BBC. He lives near Oxford, England with his wife and daughter.

Bruce Henry,
Presiding Clerk,
Australia Yearly Meeting
July 2025

© THE RELIGIOUS SOCIETY OF FRIENDS (QUAKERS) IN AUSTRALIA, 2025
PRODUCED BY THE RELIGIOUS SOCIETY OF FRIENDS (QUAKERS) IN AUSTRALIA INC.

DOWNLOAD FROM QUAKERSAUSTRALIA.INFO/RESOURCES/BACKHOUSE-LECTURES
OR ORDER FROM IPOZ.BIZ/SHOP
YOUTUBE.COM/@QUAKERSAUSTRALIA

THE JAMES *BACKHOUSE* LECTURES

2002 *To Do Justly, and to Love Mercy: Learning from Quaker Service*, Mark Deasey

2003 *Respecting the Rights of Children and Young People: A New Perspective on Quaker Faith and Practice*, Helen Bayes

2004 *Growing Fruitful Friendship: A Garden Walk*, Ute Caspers

2005 *Peace is a Struggle*, David Johnson

2006 *One Heart and a Wrong Spirit: The Religious Society of Friends and Colonial Racism*, Polly O Walker

2007 *Support for Our True Selves: Nurturing the Space Where Leadings Flow*, Jenny Spinks

2008 *Faith, Hope and Doubt in Times of Uncertainty: Combining the Realms of Scientific and Spiritual Inquiry*, George Ellis

2009 *The Quaking Meeting: Transforming Our Selves, Our Meetings and the More than-human World*, Helen Gould

2010 *Finding our voice: Our truth, community and journey as Australian Young Friends*, Australian Young Friends

2011 *A demanding and uncertain adventure: Exploration of a concern for Earth restoration and how we must live to pass on to our children*, Rosemary Morrow

2012 *From the inside out: Observations on Quaker work at the United Nations*, David Atwood

2013 *A Quaker astronomer reflects: Can a scientist also be religious?* Jocelyn Bell Burnell

2014 *'Our life is love, and peace, and tenderness': Bringing children into the centre of Quaker life and worship*, Tracy Bourne

2015 *'This we can do': Quaker faith in action through the Alternatives to Violence Project*, Sally Herzfeld

2016 *Everyday prophets*, Margery Post Abbott

2017 *Reflections on the 50th anniversary of the 1967 Referendum in the context of two Aboriginal life stories*, David Carline and Cheryl Buchanan

2018 *An Encounter between Quaker Mysticism and Taoism in Everyday Life*, Cho-Nyon Kim

2019 *Animating freedom: Accompanying Indigenous struggles for self-determination*, Jason MacLeod

2020 *Seeking union with spirit: Experiences of spiritual journeys*, Fiona Gardner

2022 *Creating Hope: Working for justice in catastrophic times*, Yarrow Woodley

2023 *Quakers, the Internet, and What's Next*, Jon Watts

2024 *God's ways, not our ways: A dissident Quaker response to disability*, Jackie Leach Scully

2025
THE JAMES BACKHOUSE LECTURE

The seed is in all: A journey through the Quaker world

Tim Gee

'One generation goes and another comes, yet the word and power and spirit of the living God endures forever, and is the same and never changes.'
– Margaret Fell

© 2025 Religious Society of Friends (Quakers) in Australia
PO Box 6063, O'Connor ACT 2602
coordinator@quakersaustralia.info
quakersaustralia.org.au

ISBN 978-1923435-08-7 (PB); ISBN 978-1923435-09-4 (Ebk)

© 2025, Tim Gee, The Religious Society of Friends (Quakers) in Australia

The moral rights of the author have been asserted.

All rights reserved. Except as permitted under the *Australian Copyright Act 1968* (for example, a fair dealing for the purposes of study, research, criticism or review), no part of this book may be reproduced, stored in a retrieval system, communicated or transmitted in any form or by any means without prior written permission.

Design & layout by:
Interactive Publications Pty Ltd, Carindale, Queensland 4152

Cover image: Marcela Teran/Liberation Works.

A catalogue record for this book is available from the National Library of Australia

Contents

Acknowledgements	vi
About the Author	vii
Introduction	1
Openings	5
International Quakerism	11
Engaging with difference	17
Sexual Diversity	19
Use of the Bible	20
The Epistle of James	23
James and Early Quakers	27
Points of Convergence	31
Growing points	35
Some Predictions	39
Queries	43
Conclusion	45

Acknowledgements

I would like to acknowledge the encouragement and mentorship of Simon C Lamb, late clerk of the FWCC Central Executive Committee, whose last words to me consisted of an email offering heartfelt encouragement to deliver the present text.

His one request was that, when listing the ways in which Friends today engage with scripture, I include those who study and cherish the Bible not as a rule book, but as a way of understanding how God and humanity have engaged throughout history, as suggested by Robert Barclay.

The email finished with:
"I pray that the Holy Spirit may empower the message to those who listen.
Your Friend,
Simon"

About the Author

Tim Gee is the General Secretary of Friends World Committee for Consultation (FWCC), which connects Quakers in different countries. He has previously worked for Britain Yearly Meeting, Christian Aid and Amnesty International. He has written four books: *Counterpower: Making Change Happen* (2011), *You Can't Evict an Idea: What can we learn from Occupy?* (2012), *Why I am a Pacifist* (2018) and *Open for Liberation: An activist reads the Bible* (2022). He contributes regularly to various publications and has been a voice for Quakers on the BBC. He lives near Oxford, England with his wonderful wife and daughter.

Introduction

I began preparing this lecture two years ago, on my goodbye visit to the Woodbrooke Quaker Study Centre in England. As for many Friends in Britain and beyond, it's a place that has given me a sense of connection with both my own family history and the wider family of Friends. It also played a major role in the development of the type of Quakerism that helped form my spiritual worldview.

My favourite place there was the library where you could go looking for one thing and end up finding ten others. It hosted the journals of the eminent and not-so-eminent Quakers in whose footsteps we follow. And, in those books—some of them hundreds of years old—it would be common to find annotations from the likes of the Rowntrees or the Cadburys who had helped to found Woodbrooke in the first place.

I was there to look for some of the works of James Backhouse, after whom this lecture series is named. Without much searching, I found what I was looking for, including a summary of his visits to South Africa and Australia, to where I would later travel.

The first thing I noticed in those dense and detailed accounts was that the spiritual and the mundane sat side by side with no real distinction between the two. So, Friends, if you find anything I have to say today mundane, please take it as in the spirit of Backhouse's writing and search for the profound within it.

The second, closely related, was the way that Backhouse and others saw scripture in almost everything, and could reach for it so easily. That's consistent with the parts of Quakerism growing fastest today, for example in East Africa or South America.

For those of us who live in increasingly secular countries—usually the Friends who practice the silent, unprogrammed form of worship—there's often not that sort of Biblical literacy anymore. Instead, we might more readily seek inspiration from Quaker tradition or even from sources which, on the face of it, might not seem religious at all, such as poetry, art or nature.

I see these two strands becoming increasingly divergent: the one primarily referencing scripture, and the other principally finding inspiration from elsewhere. In the course of this lecture, I would like to play a part in bringing them back together, aided of course by the Spirit which connects all things.

In continuation of the Quaker method of sharing testimony from personal experience, I'm going to share something about my faith journey, then try to paint a picture of our international community of Friends, before sharing some predictions about where we might be heading.

But first I want to share what I was feeling as I first sat down to write.

After reading Backhouse's words for a while, I stopped and sat. Then I looked up, looked around me, and then looked inwards. There I was: in Woodbrooke library, soon to close its doors for the last time, surrounded by the works of our predecessors. I was feeling grateful to them, but also acknowledging that the writers of most of these books have gone. It's important to say that Woodbrooke lives on as an online-first international learning charity, reaching people in many more countries than they could when largely connected to a building. But, at that point, it still felt symbolic that Woodbrooke Quaker Study centre, this bricks and mortar symbol of liberal Quakerism, would soon be gone, too.

I felt a need to recognise that the things, places or people we might think would always be there, 'safe as houses', won't always be there— and now it's us. Part of that us is me, and you, and everybody here. It's down to us to work out how to interpret, 'remix' and reimagine Quakerism for our and the next generation's needs.

And then I thought about my work with the Friends World Committee for Consultation, which connects Quakers in 100+ countries. Through that, I can see that Quakerism worldwide is energetic, dynamic, international, diverse and making change for peace. It's also growing. In my lifetime, the number of Quakers in the world has doubled from around 200,000 when I was a child, to 400,000 at the last count.

Please hold that encouragement with you, to which I would like to add that I feel profoundly positive about the Society of Friends. We will have a future for as long as God has a purpose for us, and for as long as Friends seek to unite our lives with that purpose.

And so I began to write.

Openings

My story begins in Britain, which is the Quaker community in which I grew up, and the Yearly Meeting I am a member of. Recently, as part of 'Quaker Week', one of the 'asks' was to share words that might help encourage families to try out a Quaker meeting for the first time, or indeed to stay.

I did not find that hard. I feel immensely grateful to have been a child in the Quaker community, as it helped give me a basis to try and navigate the world.

If you know me well, you might not be surprised to know that as a child I was diagnosed as hyperactive, or with ADHD, as it's usually called today. Thanks to fairly regular Quaker meetings for worship, though, I can sit still. I'm comfortable with silence and enjoy it. I probably fidget with my phone more than I should, but I'd like to think I'm not entirely dependent on it, thanks to that childhood foundation of learning to value space and stillness.

I also grew up knowing people who were committed to peace and justice, often making change against the odds after sticking at it for decades. They would (usually) be very modest about it and tell stories about Quaker change-makers of the past who inspired them. But, no matter what a Friend's age might be or what they had achieved, they treated me an equal, which felt unusual and empowering.

So, I learnt to treat adults and authority figures with respect but not deference. This sometimes got me into trouble, especially with people in positions of power who believe that respect and deference are one and the same. But there it is: our modern equivalent of those early Friends who refused to take their hats off for the king.

That was very different to school, not only with the teachers, but also with the students. There was a lot of pressure to conform: to wear certain kinds of clothes, eat certain kinds of foods, even have certain colours of hair. If you didn't fit in, you'd be bullied; if you stood up to bullies, you got in the firing line. So, I didn't like school.

I got through it, partly thanks to Quaker youth events at weekends and in the holidays, which were a complete contrast: they were joyful safe spaces where we could explore and experiment with our identities and beliefs, knowing that we would be welcomed and loved just the same.

What I didn't have was very much religious language to interpret this. In my mum's Quaker school, the head of Religious Education believed that, if you instruct children in the Bible, they will form a childlike picture of it, which will need to be unlearned later on in life. Better then to explore and to model good values, illustrated by Bible stories here and there. Then, when people find their way to scripture, they'll appreciate it first time around.

That is pretty much what happened for me. Today, I recognise the presence of God in every good experience, then and now, but that's not how I would have put it at the time. Today, too, I have a very positive relationship with the Bible, and with Jesus manifested as the inward Light and Guide. This kind of language is much to the surprise of some of my friends, who did indeed reject a religious worldview early on.

I almost rejected it, too. Some of the Christians I met at school, for example, said things that really didn't sound right, such as my parents were going to go to hell because they were divorced, and I was going to hell because I hadn't had water sprinkled on my head as a baby, and that would be the case however good a life I lived. Unsurprisingly, I found it quite repellent.

Then, a Christian Prime Minister of the UK joined a Christian President of the United States in ordering the invasion of Afghanistan and Iraq, leading to hundreds of thousands of deaths, and I thought Christians had very strange priorities.

But I didn't switch off from faith altogether. Quakers were solid in their opposition to those wars, and through that movement I learnt that, when you know something isn't right very deep in your heart, then that still small voice needs to be listened to.

I studied politics with an international focus, in the hope that understanding the systems through which violence is perpetrated might equip me to do something about it. I was impressed with Thomas Paine's books on human rights and carried on from there to his book on religion, the *Age of Reason*.

It's a well-argued book including a memorable section on the meaning of direct religious experience, in which he declares that, while he would never dispute or deny someone else's revelations, nobody should be obliged to believe such reports unless they happen to them. Built in to my enjoyment of this passage was a fairly complacent assumption that God was very unlikely to speak to me.

Then, in the middle of a meeting for worship in Philadelphia, something changed. I recognised that the flow of love and Light flowing through all people's hearts also flows through me. It was an ecstatic experience. I quaked. It wasn't a revelation in words, but it did make religious words start making sense: like 1 John 4:8 "God is Love", and George Fox's moment of revelation: "I saw also that there was… an infinite ocean of Light… in that also I saw the infinite love of God".

I went home and applied for membership. And, thanks to a prompt from a wise and gentle elder in my meeting, I also started engaging with the Bible more seriously, beginning with the *Book of James* which I'll come back to later.

International Quakerism

Because this convincement experience took place away from my home country, since then, I've thought of my Quakerism as international, rather than bounded by borders, even if my local meeting was and still is in Britain. A decade later, when many meetings started going online, especially thanks to pandemic restrictions, I started taking part in Quaker Meetings in other places from my sofa: first in Europe, then North America, Latin America and East Africa, eventually reaching the other side of the world with Friends here in Asia West Pacific.

And, well, it's not hard to see that some of the worship styles in global Quakerism are very different. Compare the singing and dancing and three-hour services in Kenya with the mostly silent gatherings in Britain, Australia and various other parts of the world.

But I was welcomed everywhere: not quizzed about my beliefs, not tested on whether I knew the words to the songs, but warmly and meaningfully welcomed like a long-lost family member. More than anything else, I believe that this kind of welcome is key to our flourishing.

And now I work for the Friends World Committee for Consultation, which brings together people from these different ways of worshipping. However we worship, I am always reminded of Jesus' words in Matthew: "Where two or three are gathered in my name, there I am in the midst of them".

I could speak for a long time about the variety of religious experiences in Quakerism, which is almost infinite, endlessly fascinating and gives plenty to think about in all their complexity and nuance. But I'll try to not dwell on them too much. Instead, I'd like to speak about the things we have in common. They are relatively few, but as such are pleasingly simple.

One is a direct unmediated relationship with the Divine (although the meanings people attach to the word divine vary greatly). Another is our shared history. And a third is our work for justice with peace, which takes place in different ways in different places.

There are probably other things too, but they are more subtle. For example, meeting houses and Friends Churches are usually simple, not covered with gold. People tend to dress relatively simply. There's the whole Quaker language of clerks and monthly meetings, which is beautifully familiar around the world. Women being in leadership is normal and accepted, which is different from some of our Christian neighbours for whom this is either disallowed or still new. Among Quaker men, there's also something I recognise and try to do: model being male without being macho.

Then there are the differences, which are glorious. At the Friends Church in Bujumbura, one of the largest in the world, up to nine choirs sing together on a Sunday morning. At another church in Burundi on the site of a Friends school, the voices were so full when I visited, I thought I saw the walls shaking.

This is a major contrast to silent meetings, without doubt. But inwardly there is also an extraordinary connection, because when I sing with Quakers who sing, I feel the same strong divine connection that I feel in a still and silent meeting for worship. Our connections are from the inside out.

Other things seem like differences but are in fact similar. On occasion in Kenya, I've been asked to give a sermon. I've never been asked to do that in an unprogrammed meeting, but I have been asked to give prepared ministry, like today. The process of preparation for both of these is very similar.

Friends accustomed to unprogrammed meetings for worship sometimes express concern that a church with a pastor might not be fully participative. I would respond that, when I have taken part in Friends Church services, many different groups have a go at the front: perhaps the children might do a skit, the teenagers might do a dance, various people would share testimonies and women and men of all ages will speak, which is more than can be said for what happens in unprogrammed meetings. On a day like World Quaker Day, this might all happen at once, or, on ordinary days, there might be a rotation with different groups leading services each week. So, let's put to bed the idea that programmed services can't be participatory.

On the other hand, a Friend accustomed to programmed worship might express a concern that the lack of many prepared words in unprogrammed Quakerism might lead to a rather vague or nebulous theology. Well, theology literally means the study of God. Silent worship is a way of experiencing God within and among us without many words. Words can point us towards God, but they can also distort or distract especially if they become legalistic or stultified. So, 'silent worship Quakers' do theology. A gathered meeting for worship is a process of encounter with the Divine, of studying the Divine with the heart.

You could call this a kind of 'silent theology', through which we can reach what my granny called a kind of wordless knowing.

So, it's good that people are concerned about one another and are asking questions. It's also good that there are answers, and that we can learn from each other. A wordless knowing is a profound and wonderful thing. A largely silent theology, though, isn't at all sustainable, as we've always known.

Accordingly, from the start, Friends have sought words to communicate our faith. The words have changed over time, and in different places. I hold faith that the divine experience at the heart of it remains the same.

Engaging with difference

I've mentioned some of our differences, like forms of worship, but these are probably the easier ones. With a shared theology, variations in worship styles are relatively straightforward to stomach, often more a matter of preference than underlying values.

Some of our differences are harder, though, and I've been asked to talk about these, too. So, amid all this talk of unity, it's important to say that some of our differences are significant. But, in this divided and increasingly polarised world, surely being cordial with and curious about people we might disagree with is part of the practice of peace. Our global faith community gives us opportunities to hone those skills.

I'm going to mention two: sexual diversity and approaches to the Bible.

Sexual Diversity

Quaker takes on sexual diversity vary widely around the world. It's important not to characterise all people from a particular country or particular yearly meeting as having a unified view. There are nuances and differences on these questions within countries and yearly meetings. Nevertheless, official teaching and books of faith and practice in some countries very much embrace LGBTQI+ affirming Christianity, whereas others very much don't.

At the most recent World Plenary Meeting, we acknowledged together that sexual discrimination and disunity over sexual orientation continue to hold us back. On some level, I hope that the process of meeting with one another and building connections in the things we do have in common, whilst speaking from experience about the things that we don't, does make a difference on some level. But it is a slow process.

If it's any consolation, we are in much the same position as almost all other Christian World Communions, who also struggle with this. It can help us humble ourselves to know we are not so different from our

Christian brothers and sisters in this regard. Of course, we consider Quakerism to be special, but we're not so special as to have found a way through this one, except to handle the conversation with civility and respect as much as possible.

It is even more humbling to consider that the Quaker takes on sexuality around the world tend to be pretty much in line with, or perhaps only a little ahead of, social attitudes more generally in those countries.[1] That opens the possibility that our respective positions are less a product of scriptural exegesis or direct revelation, as a product of the cultures we are in. In some ways this is a troubling idea, and I realise it's unlikely to please anyone. As a means to understanding one another, though, I think it can be helpful.

I wish I could offer a succinct reflection to sum up this section, but the truth is, it remains an unresolved, uncomfortable, untidy tension in the world community of Friends, just as it is in the world community as a whole. I hope you will join me in prayer that God will lead us in a way through.

Use of the Bible

A second set of differences relates to approaches to the Bible and theism more broadly. These are the modern manifestations of some of the major historic splits that have centred on disputes about the primacy of scripture against the primacy of experiencing the Holy Spirit. Is the Bible the literal Word of God, or is The Word that powerful but inexpressible Spirit that was in the beginning, for which words will always be inadequate?

Back in 1678, Robert Barclay characterised the Bible as "a faithful historical account of the actings of God's people", "a prophetical account of several things, whereof some are already past, and some yet to come", and "a full and ample account of all the chief principles of the doctrine of Christ". He then famously added that it is "a declaration of the fountain, and not the fountain itself" and a "secondary rule,

---

[1] On the face of it, the principal exception to this would appear to be the USA, where views are very polarised. Differences within or between yearly meetings reflect this.

subordinate to the Spirit, from which they have all their excellency and certainty".

Over the years, different Quaker groupings in different places have emphasised different parts of this standpoint, leading to the extraordinary spectrum we have today: from some Friends holding that the Bible is the only source of truth, through to a midpoint in which the Bible is a companion to contemplation, right through to the other extreme where the Bible is a book of off-putting God-language, or even an instrument of oppression, best left alone.

There are still Friends today who, as Barclay suggested, see scripture not as a rule book but as a way of understanding how God and humanity have engaged throughout history, and who study and cherish the Bible because of that. My Friend Simon Lamb, late clerk of FWCC, was one of them, and in his last email to me said his one request for this lecture was to include Friends who hold this position.

I've had different views at different times, and as such have an empathy for different perspectives. At one point, if I'd have come across the word non-theist, I may well have described myself as one, although I was never quite an atheist since I always held open the possibility of God. Through reading the Bible, though, I moved to a place where I felt led to write a book about the scriptures as a tool of liberation.

From the perspective of working for FWCC, an organisation that seeks to bring together Friends from different cultures, traditions and countries, I find myself harbouring a deep desire for shared Bible study to help us understand one another across our differences as well as to connect with the words that helped inspire Quakerism in the first place, too, and so rediscover the radicalism of our forebears.

The Epistle of James

I mentioned that my doorway to the Bible was the Epistle of James, which I'd like to talk more about now.

I'm reliably informed that, based on the written evidence we have from early Friends, the reason we are known as we are is in part because of the use of the word Friend in the Epistle of James.

There are more reasons Friends might be drawn to this part of the Bible. Quakers in our origins sought to be the early Church revived. James was the earliest leader of the Church following the earthly life of Jesus. Others call Quakerism 'New Testament Christianity done well'. It's possible that James was the earliest text of the New Testament to be written.

He also definitely existed. Many Liberal Friends take an interest in the kinds of questions raised by historical-critical approaches to the Bible, like asking which figures and stories can be verified by historical sources. Although scholars will question almost any ancient text, James shows up in so many that there is no reason to doubt that he existed. He is mentioned in the Gospels, Acts and letters of Paul, as well as the works of Josephus, Eusebius, and Hegesippus.

From these sources we know he was vegetarian and a teetotaller, which would be a point of unity with many (although by no means all) Friends. Vegetarianism is much more common among unprogrammed Quakers. Abstention from alcohol is the norm among Friends in East Africa.

He's also literally Jesus' brother. Given Jesus didn't leave behind any text that we know of, the words of his brother who knew him all his life can help bring us closer. The fact James' letter so closely echoes Jesus' words as reported in the gospels—especially in the Sermon on the Mount—helps give weight to the historicity of both. Both speak strongly about peace and justice.

Yet, the Epistle of James has often been marginalised, overlooked or ignored through the centuries, largely because of the ways his message was inconvenient to some other forms of theology. Well, Quakers love being inconvenient, especially in pursuit of peace and justice, and have an empathy for the marginalised. So, here's another reason to engage.

In James, we find a theology of action—perhaps even of activism—in which he says that "faith by itself, if it does not result in action, is dead", "I will show you my faith by my deeds", "faith without deeds is worthless", and then again, "faith without deeds is dead"; that religion that God accepts is to "look after orphans and widows in their distress"; and that instead of talking all the time, we should be "doers of the Word".

In different translations, the resonances with Quaker terms are extraordinary. As I mentioned before, James uses the word "Friend", saying that we become a Friend of God by what we do, and that friendship with the world (meaning the unjust systems of the world) is enmity with God.[2] In some translations, gatherings for worship are described as meetings.[3] Parts of it sound like advice for an unprogrammed meeting: like the guidance to "bridle the tongue", be "quick to listen, slow to speak" and to "welcome with meekness the implanted word".

Nowadays, English-speaking Friends often speak of the SPICES (Simplicity, Peace, Integrity, Community, Equality and Sustainability). Again, it's all there. Simplicity: a whole chapter of James is a warning to rich oppressors. Peace: James reaffirms the commandment not to kill. Integrity: This is where we get the line much quoted by Friends, "let your yay be yay and nay be nay" (let your yes be yes and your no be no). Community: James reminds us to love our neighbour. Equality: he says that all should be treated equally in our meetings, regardless of wealth or poverty. Finally, Sustainability or Stewardship: James gives us a warning against greed, which can lead to war and destruction.

Also like his brother Jesus, James says nothing at all about same sex relationships and—unlike his contemporary and occasional rival Paul—says nothing that could be misconstrued as support for slavery or gender inequality.

---

[2] In the Gospel According to John, Jesus famously said "Ye are my Friends if ye do whatsoever I command you"–an important text for Friends in many countries. I am told, though, that where early Friends found a scriptural basis for the word Friend, it was from James.

[3] Including the NIV and NLT among others, but not the KJV, which implies that this is not the origin of the Quaker use of the word.

James and Early Quakers

Once I had read it a few times, I started noticing how many of the widely cited quotes from Quaker tradition in turn cite the epistle of James. For example, George Fox's famous claim, to live "in the virtue of that life and power that takes away the occasion of all wars", speaks in the same sentence of what he calls "James's doctrine" that wars arise from greed in the heart.

In Margaret Fell's articulation of the peace testimony, she cites the epistle of James to explain why Quakers don't swear oaths, why Quakers don't fight with outward weapons, and why Quakers seek to treat people as equals. She then goes on to say that the only ground and cause of Quakers' sufferings is because Friends obeyed the Command of Christ and observed James' teaching.[4]

John Woolman's "a caution to the rich" echoes James in its title; the final chapter of James's epistle is often headed, "A warning to the rich". The alternate title of Woolman's essay is "A Plea for the Poor". I don't know if Woolman would have been aware of it or not, but there is a connection here, too. The followers of James were called the Ebionites, which in English translates as *The Poor*.

Clearly, then, whether we know it or not, there has been a resonance over time with those early Quaker writings that channel James. That got me interested in whether early Friends quoted James any more than any other comparable New Testament letter. So, I counted up references from George Fox and others using Earlham College's *Quaker Bible Index*, and discovered that, no, they don't.

My breakthrough moment came from revisiting Barclay's *Apology*. Deep within that, Barclay says that even in his time other churches were restricting the reading of James, while Quakers, assured by the Spirit, embraced it as a full and equal part of scripture. It follows then that in doing so Quakers developed in some ways that were distinctive.

---
[4] Fell's words are "the apostle's doctrine and practice". In context, it's clear that the apostle referenced here is James, probably referring to church teaching of the past that the apostle James and the brother of Christ are the same person.

Even if early Friends didn't cite James more than other parts of the Bible, it's likely they did read it more than some of their Christian contemporaries.

I mentioned before that the epistle is inconvenient to some other forms of theology, but it's worth pausing here to consider why this might have been. James' unmistakable condemnation of inequality and war was inconvenient for those forms of Christianity that perpetuated inequality and war. His instruction that rich men not be given special seats didn't really sit well with emperors and kings on their thrones, neither did lines like "the rich will be humbled", "the rich will disappear", or "the rich will wither away". James' role as the leader of the more Jewish branch of early Christianity was inconvenient for the Roman Church when it was seeking to distance itself from Judaism.

James' bold, rather stark and repeated statements about faith and works were inconvenient for Martin Luther and for Calvinists, who argued for justification by faith alone. (This wasn't inconvenient for Barclay, who said faith and works could go together.) Plus, of course, the very existence of James as Jesus' brother was very inconvenient indeed to any church that promulgated the doctrine of Mary's perpetual virginity, for obvious reasons.

It may have been marginalised, and tucked in towards the end, but the Book of James is still there, in our Bibles, on our meeting house tables, on our bookshelves and our lecterns, ready to be re-embraced.

For Bible-based Friends in churches with pastors and programmed worship, this is a Bible book that could help explain why some Friends are as they are.

For unprogrammed Friends, especially Friends who perhaps might feel hesitant about expressing themselves with the aid of scripture, it could be a great starting point in doing so.

So, if there is one thing you do after listening to or reading this lecture, I'd like to invite you to open a Bible at the Epistle of James and see what you get from it.

Points of Convergence

Something I have always loved about Quakers is the idea that we are always on a journey together, and each conversation along the way can help change our ideas about the world. To converge doesn't mean to stay in the same place.

I've found myself on a perpetual journey, and along the way have discovered a newfound appreciation for aspects of Christian practice that weren't a major part of my upbringing.

I'm not saying that all the kinds of Quakerism need to re-merge, or that our mission should be to seek a kind of spiritual midpoint between the different traditions. I don't think that's possible or desirable.

What I do hope is that, especially in this age of global internet communication, we could learn a lot more from one another across countries, cultures and Quaker traditions. For my part, I will do what I can to support FWCC to facilitate that.

We could also adapt and adopt practices that are working elsewhere, understanding them as authentically Quaker, even if they are different from the ways we are familiar with. For example, originally from the USA, the Alternatives to Violence Project is huge in East Africa, thanks to sharing and learning across borders.

I still find I love and need the peace of an unprogrammed largely silent Quaker meeting in my life. At the same time, the Spirit I've felt in Africa and elsewhere remains with me, too, and, even if my voice isn't up to much, my soul cries out to sing. I enjoyed having a hand in the most recent version of the *World Quaker Songbook*, and, in contemplative moments, I've found myself setting Bible verses to folk tunes in my journal. Some of these are included as an appendix in the written version to this lecture, or, if you are listening to this at Australia Yearly Meeting, I'll be sharing those in a workshop tomorrow.

Partly thanks to time spent with Quakers in the majority world, spoken prayer is also now a part of my life in a way it didn't used to be. And, even if not so well as Backhouse and his peers, I feel myself ready to reach for scripture in the everyday whilst also reaching for the inexpressible Spirit. In the process I feel something happening within me that feels new and renewing, yet connects me with something much older—indeed which is older than time.

Growing points

I will say again, Quakers will have a future for as long as God has a purpose for us, and so long as we unite with that purpose. Right now, we are growing. In fact, there are quite possibly more Quakers alive today than at any other time.

One of the questions I am asked most often in places where our numbers are decreasing is what we can learn from places where they aren't.

Recently, I had the pleasure of being part of a service in Nairobi, welcoming some of the 500 new Quakers coming into membership that day, following completion of the two-part course Friends in Kenya do before becoming full members.

Friends, it was such a joyful occasion. It was long—five hours—but it was joyful because we were celebrating the hard work and faithful commitment made by so many people. People danced into meeting, and we clapped and sang to them, to one another, and to God.

By my presence, I was glad to affirm these Friends entering not only a local, monthly or yearly meeting, but a global community of faith. I'm also glad to relay the joy of that occasion here, and say, Friends, the rest of the world has something to learn.

I can't help but compare it with the moment I learnt my Quaker membership had been confirmed. I was sitting in my bedroom looking at a letter through the post. My first response was a sense of anti-climax. For sure, it helped me learn that being a Quaker isn't all mountain-top moments. But, still, I think we could be better at welcoming people.

I also can't help but compare the Kenyan system of offering a free course ahead of membership to the liberal Quaker assumption that people will just absorb Quakerism by coming to meetings, sitting in silence and chatting to people afterwards, when we know that, in fact, many people don't absorb Quakerism and remain attenders forever, or alternatively form a view of Quakerism shaped by the luck of with whom they happened to be speaking that day. I'm convinced Quakers in Kenya have something good going on, which is ripe for adaption and adoption elsewhere.

And Kenya might not even be where Quaker numbers are growing fastest. They may well be growing even faster elsewhere in East Africa. I asked a Friend in Burundi why he thought the faith was growing so much there and what Friends in other countries could learn from that. Without missing a beat, he replied that firstly Quakers are democratic, which is relatively unusual for a church. (Quakers in Burundi do have a voting system, which is very interesting, but which I won't get in to here.)

He also said that, when you become a Quaker, your life gets better. Well. that's a different case for Quakerism to what I've heard before. Is *your* life better for being a Quaker? I hope it is. Mine is, and that was the case before I accepted my current job. I can think of several times the Society of Friends has been there to catch me when I could easily have fallen down. We could be more forthcoming about the ways our lives are better because of Friends. There are various ways we could do that, but it begins simply by thinking and then trying to say out loud how being part of Quakerism has made each of our lives better.

Some Predictions

Now, since this lecture is going to be printed and published, one of the dangers is you can't then go back and edit it. I'm going to feel the fear and do it anyway, though, and make some predictions for where Quakerism could be headed. I'm going to keep these relatively short, because the more I say the more likely I am to be wrong.

First of all, the Quaker centre of gravity has already moved to the Global South, which is likely to be formalised in the coming decades. As mainstream Quakerism is increasingly understood as Global South Quakerism, Global North Quakerism will be increasingly shaped by it.

Secondly, online connections will become an even bigger part of our lives, including our faith lives. As they do, the distinctions between the traditions contained by place-based yearly meetings will continue to be blurred as online inter-visitation becomes more straightforward.

Thirdly, English will no longer be the default language of international Quakerism, nor the principal language Quaker texts are written in ready for translation. I think we'll see a lot more translation of Quaker texts into English, for example, and increased language equality in the way we work.

Fourthly, and this is going to be the hardest thing for me to say, I think liberal Quakerism in its current form will pass. By that, I don't mean that we will die out. What I mean is that, through the perpetual process of change, what we currently call liberal Quakerism will change.

There have always been different eras of Quakerism. Liberal Quakerism has been around for about a century and indeed is very different now to how it was when it began. I think it's helpful to begin contemplating now, how you might like the next era to look, and what you can do to help build it.

Queries

The lecture committee has asked me to suggest some queries to aid reflection. I'm grateful for the encouragement to do so and would like to offer the following:

1. What does it mean to you to be part of a world family of Friends?
2. How do you welcome newcomers in your meeting? Could anything be improved?
3. Do you think the Epistle of James could help facilitate understanding across different forms of Quakerism?
4. Are there insights or practices from Quakers in other parts of the world which you would like to be part of your faith life?
5. How is your life better for being a Quaker?

Conclusion

I started writing this lecture two years ago in Woodbrooke library and the body of it on a long train journey to Hungary to visit Friends there. I finished it in January 2025, against the background of unfolding events in the USA, mirrored in many other countries.

Friends, in a world where environmental breakdown, war, misinformation, loneliness and unfairness seem to dominate, I am convinced that our message of simplicity, peace, integrity, community and equality is needed more than ever. Even when things seem overwhelming or unfamiliar, we can hold faith that the truths we have long held dear are an antidote to many of the problems of the world.

I don't think Quakers will fix all of these problems, but I do believe, deep in my heart, that whatever positive change comes, will need to include—indeed be led by—a collective inward change, which falls outside the current bounds of social science.

Political parties won't do this, NGOs won't do this, the media won't do this—though they might all play their part. Understanding and promoting this inward change is the realm of faith. Some people call it the voice of conscience. In religious terms, it is the Light of Christ.

In my work, I see evidence day by day that the Light shines in the dark, and the darkness has not overcome it. This will continue to be the case for as long as Friends live up to the measure of the Light given to us and also support others to do so.

I don't believe that the Light, faithfully followed, can lead people to wilfully and knowingly commit acts of harm. I do believe that it will lead us, and could lead everyone, to love God and love our neighbour. Ultimately, this principle, which Jesus said summed up all God's teaching, has within it what we and humanity as a whole need.

And I'm sure we've all noticed with deep concern the way that powerful figures are cloaking their acts in the language of religion even whilst using language designed to make us hate our neighbour.

Friends, someone needs to stand up and say this is not the way of Christ. It is our role to do so.

All the evidence shows that there are thousands, possibly millions, of people waiting to be reached, sensing a profound inward spirituality but searching for a community to help them interpret it. Please help them find us, rather than be attracted to wolves in sheep's clothing.

The world needs what Quakers have to offer, not for our survival as a Society of Friends, but for the survival of the values we promote and for the better world they lead to. Quakerism is a precious patch of ground in the landscape of faith, sometimes a place of refuge, and a place which deserves to be nurtured and known for welcoming people, and speaking truth to power.

That begins with channelling the energy of our forebears and Friends around the world. It means getting out and telling people we're here, they are welcome, and to paraphrase George Fox's final words, that the spirit of God, the seed of Christ, is in all and over all. With Friends, folk can find it.

So, yes. Some things change. Change is happening all the time. But the insights at the heart of our faith do not.

When I started writing this talk in the Woodbrooke library, the first words I wrote at the top of my page were from Margaret Fell, and it's with these words that I'd like to finish:

"*The truth is one and the same always, though ages and generations pass away. And as One generation goes and another comes, yet the Word and Power and Spirit of the living God endures forever, and is the same and never changes.*"

Notes on the Text

As this was written as a lecture rather than as an essay, I have tried my best to avoid filling it with references or footnotes, except where I thought they were necessary to clarify a point. As it is also due to be published, though, this note is offered as a replacement.

I have found the *New Living Translation* the most accessible of the mainstream Bible translations, the *King James Version* the most familiar, and the *New Revised Standard Version* (Updated Edition) the most agreeable. I am currently greatly appreciating the recent *First Nations Version*.

My preference has been for an 'immersion' approach—either reading or listening to larger sections at a time. In a similar spirit, I have sought to weave Biblical references and allusions into the narrative rather than drawing out 'proof texts'.

Where I have focussed on individual passages, I've found online tools like Bible Gateway very useful for comparing the many different translations. I have long found the advice attributed to Augustine helpful, that, if any text in the Bible appears on the surface to contradict Jesus' command to love God and our neighbour, we should contemplate on it until an interpretation emerges which points towards the rule of charity.

Quotes from George Fox and Margaret Fell can be found in Britain Yearly Meeting's *Quaker Faith and Practice* and elsewhere.

Robert Barclay's *An Apology for the True Christian Divinity* is available on FriendsLibrary.com, and the Project Gutenberg website among others, whilst the *Age of Reason* is on the website of the Thomas Paine National Historical Association. These online versions are especially easily navigable.

Hegesippus' description of James is quoted at length in Eusebius' *Ecclesiastical History*. Josephus' mention of James is in *Antiquities of the Jews*, Book 20, Chapter 9.

The Earlham *Quaker Bible Index* is available at https://qbi.earlham.edu

The language of 'remixing' Quakerism comes from C Wess Daniels. Books include *Resisting Empire* and *A Convergent Model of Renewal*. A shorter summary is presented in a 2021 article in *Quaker Religious Thought*, titled "Revolutionary Faithfulness: Quaker Pastoral Practice and Theology in an Age of Empire".

My book about the scriptures is titled *Open for Liberation: an Activist Reads the Bible*, published in 2022 by Christian Alternative, an imprint of Collective Ink. Paulette Meier's *Timeless Quaker Wisdom in Plainsong*, including a version of the quote from Margaret Fell, is available from www.paulettemeier.com

Some fruits of contemplation

In the beginning
Tune: "Scarborough Fair"

In the beginning there was the Word
And the Word it was with God
All things were made, in Him there was Life
And the Word, it was God

He was the Light, which lighteth all
And the Word it was with God
That giveth Light to all in this world
And the Word, it was God

Though in the world, the world knew him not
And the Word it was with God
And so they hung him up on a cross
And the Word, it was God

As I consider the way Jesus died
And the Word it was with God
The Word that's in all can't stay crucified
And the Word, it was God.

Magnificat (Mary's song)
Tune: "Bella Ciao"

My heart rejoices, in God my Saviour
For he took notice of his servant girl
I have within me, the Prince of Peace
And my soul magnifies the Lord

My Lord has brought down, the high and mighty
And he has scattered the haughty and the proud,
But the humble, he has exalted
And my soul magnifies the Lord

He's filled the hungry, he shows his mercy
From now all generations will call me blessed
But the rich he sent away empty
And my soul magnifies the Lord

And my soul magnifies the Lord

Meditation (Psalm 131)
Tune: "All Through the Night"

Lord, my heart it is not haughty
Nor my eyes raised high
I don't worry about things
That I don't understand

My soul feels quiet and calmer
Like a baby with its mama
I am like the weaned child
That is with me.

The Beatitudes
Tune: "O Shenandoah"

Oh blessed are, the poor in Spirit,
For theirs is the Kingdom
Oh blessed are, all those in mourning
You're going to be, I know you're going to be
Filled with consolation

Oh blessed are, those who are humble
The earth you will inherit
Oh blessed are, those who seek justice
You're going to be, I know you're going to be
Filled with satisfaction

Oh blessed are, those who show mercy
You will be shown mercy too
Oh blessed are, those with pure hearts
You're going to see, I know you're going to see
God in the hearts of others

Oh blessed are, all the peace makers
You will be called God's children
Oh blessed are the persecuted,
You're going to be, I know you're going to be
In the Kingdom of Heaven.

Ballad of Saul/Paul
Tune: "Dives & Lazarus (Star of the County Down)"

As I went down the Damascus Road
Some Christians for to chase
Their teaching and their way of life
Was much to my distaste

And then I saw a blinding Light,
And I quaked in my surprise
"Why are you persecuting Me?"
Said the voice of Jesus Christ

So I rose and I went to a street called Straight
To the house of one called Jude
And although I neither ate nor drank
I was filled with Spiritual food

I saw the Light, and regained my sight
As I rose I was baptised
I was filled the Spirit that connects all things
And the scales fell from my eyes

On Love
Tune: "Aura Lee" ("Love me Tender")

Love is patient, Love is kind
Love does not envy
It doesn't boast, it isn't rude
Or insist on its own way

Love bears all things
Hopes all things
Helped from up above
Now faith, hope and Love abide
The-greatest it is Love

Love will never end I know
Even though tongues cease
Knowledge it will pass away
So will prophecies

Love bears all things
Hopes all things
Helped from up above
Now faith, hope and love abide
The-greatest it is Love

I used to think like a child
Now-I see in a mirror dim
Then I shall know fully when
I'm face to face with Him

Love bears all things
Hopes all things
Helped from up above
Now faith, hope and love abide
The-greatest it is Love

Epitaph (Psalm 26)
Tune: "The Water is Wide"

Bless me O Lord
For I have walked
A path of truth
And integrity

Put me on trial
Cross-examine me
For I have lived
A life of peace

I do not spend
My time with liars
I do not join
With those who harm

I don't abide
Hypocrisy
Thank you my God
For helping me

So here I stand
On solid ground
I love the place
That my God is found

Redeem me Lord
Show me your mercy
I've tried to live
Life faithfully.

www.ingramcontent.com/pod-product-compliance
Lightning Source LLC
Chambersburg PA
CBHW070107100426
42743CB00012B/2674